AF228621

HOUSTON ROCKETS

BY WILL GRAVES

SportsZone

An Imprint of Abdo Publishing
abdobooks.com

abdobooks.com

Published by Abdo Publishing, a division of ABDO, PO Box 398166, Minneapolis, Minnesota 55439. Copyright © 2023 by Abdo Consulting Group, Inc. International copyrights reserved in all countries. No part of this book may be reproduced in any form without written permission from the publisher. SportsZone™ is a trademark and logo of Abdo Publishing.

Printed in China
052022
092022

Cover Photo: Noah K. Murray/AP Images
Interior Photos: Melinda Nagy/Shutterstock Images, 1; Pat Sullivan/AP Images, 4, 10, 20; Rick Bowmer/AP Images, 6, 9, 29; Ira Strickstein/Houston Chronicle/AP Images, 13; AP Images, 14; Focus on Sport/Getty Images, 16, 24, 26, 34; Bettmann/Getty Images, 19; Simon M. Bruty/Anychance/Getty Images Sport/Getty Images, 21; Marcio Jose Sanchez/AP Images, 23; Tim Johnson/AP Images, 28; Jeff Gross/Getty Images Sport/Getty Images, 31; Scott Halleran/Getty Images Sport/Getty Images, 33; Lennox McClendon/AP Images, 36; Tim Johnson/AP Images, 37; Bob Levey/Getty Images Sport/Getty Images, 39; Noah K. Murray/AP Images, 41

Editor: Charlie Beattie
Series Designer: Joshua Olson

Library of Congress Control Number: 2021951672

Publisher's Cataloging-in-Publication Data

Names: Graves, Will, author.
Title: Houston Rockets / by Will Graves
Description: Minneapolis, Minnesota : Abdo Publishing, 2023 | Series: Inside the NBA | Includes online resources and index.
Identifiers: ISBN 9781532198281 (lib. bdg.) | ISBN 9781098271930 (ebook)
Subjects: LCSH: Houston Rockets (Basketball team)--Juvenile literature. | Basketball--Juvenile literature. | Professional sports--Juvenile literature. | Sports franchises--Juvenile literature.
Classification: DDC 796.32364--dc23

TABLE OF
CONTENTS

CHAPTER ONE

ROCKETS LAUNCH

The Houston Rockets were down to their last stand. Heading into Game 6 of the 1994 National Basketball Association (NBA) Finals, they trailed the New York Knicks 3–2. If they didn't win, the season would be over.

In front of a raucous Houston crowd, the teams had battled all night. The Rockets led by 10 points at halftime. But the Knicks were charging. At the end of the third quarter, the Rockets' lead was down to three.

The crowd at the Summit, Houston's home arena, was getting nervous. Never before had the team won an NBA title. The season had been the best in Houston's history. The fans didn't want it to slip away. Thankfully, the Rockets had "the Dream."

Hakeem Olajuwon, *left*, launches a jump shot during the 1994 NBA Finals against the New York Knicks.

Olajuwon averaged 26.9 points per game during the 1994 NBA Finals, and he had four double-doubles.

HAKEEM THE DREAM

Hakeem "the Dream" Olajuwon was a dominant 7-foot center. Born in Nigeria, Olajuwon grew up a soccer player. At age 15 he tried basketball and instantly fell in love with the game. A few years later it brought him to the University of Houston on a basketball scholarship.

Olajuwon's University of Houston teams were high-flying entertainment. There he teamed with another future NBA All-Star in guard Clyde Drexler. The Cougars threw down so many dunks the team soon had a catchy nickname. A Houston sportswriter joked they were a fraternity named "Phi Slama Jama." With Olajuwon dominating the paint, Houston went to the Final Four three years in a row, from 1982 to 1984.

The Cougars reached the national championship game in both 1983 and 1984. But both years they were beaten. The second defeat came at the hands of 7-foot-1-inch center Patrick Ewing and his Georgetown University Hoyas. The loss was Olajuwon's last college game. He left the Cougars without a title.

He wasn't going far. The Rockets had the top pick in the 1984 NBA Draft. Olajuwon was an easy choice. Now, 10 years later, he was trying to get Houston a professional basketball title. And Ewing, now the Knicks' star player, was once again standing in his way.

GAME 6 HERO

Both big men were having strong nights in Game 6. Olajuwon was Houston's main offensive weapon every night. Ewing's powerful low post moves made him a force for the Knicks. However, in the fourth quarter, one of the smallest men on the floor was stealing the show.

Knicks guard John Starks stood just 6 feet, 3 inches tall and weighed 180 pounds. But he played fearlessly. He challenged Olajuwon at the basket multiple times. Despite the size difference, Starks was winning the battles and getting layups. He was hitting his outside shots as well. With 1:20 to go, Starks drilled a three-pointer to cut Houston's lead to 84–82.

Olajuwon responded with two free throws to put Houston up by four points again. New York answered right back with a jumper from forward Anthony Mason. Thirty seconds remained, and Houston needed one more bucket. The Rockets tried to get the ball to Olajuwon. New York's tough defense wouldn't let that happen. As the shot clock ran down, guard Kenny Smith had to force up a shot with Knicks guard Derek Harper in his face. It missed.

The Knicks grabbed the rebound and called timeout. New York had 5.5 seconds left to run a play. Of course it was going to the hot-shooting Starks. The guard took the inbounds pass and ran to his left, where Ewing's screen was waiting for him. Starks curled around the big center, then hoisted a shot from

The 1994 Finals matched Olajuwon, *left*, with another of the NBA's best big men, the Knicks' Patrick Ewing, *right*.

Olajuwon races out to challenge John Starks's game-winning three-point attempt in Game 6 of the 1994 NBA Finals.

beyond the three-point line. If it went in, the Knicks would be champions.

Olajuwon read the play well. He moved away from Ewing and closed in on Starks. As the Knicks guard went up to shoot, Olajuwon extended his long right arm. The shot tipped off his fingers and came up short. Houston's star had just forced Game 7.

CHAMPIONS AT LAST

Three nights later the teams were back at it in the Summit. Again the game came down to the fourth quarter. With less than two minutes to play, Houston led by five. Olajuwon backed down Ewing, then pulled back for a jump shot. As the Rockets' center hung in the air, he changed his mind about shooting. Spotting guard Vernon Maxwell open at the three-point line, Olajuwon contorted his body to pass the ball. Maxwell's shot hit nothing but net for an 83–75 lead.

Long Time Coming

The win was a huge relief for the city of Houston's sports fans. The championship was the first major title by a Houston professional team in any major sport. The National Football League's (NFL) Houston Oilers never reached the Super Bowl before leaving for Tennessee in 1997. Baseball's Houston Astros finally won their first World Series title in 2017.

Maxwell's teammates raced to hug him as the Knicks called timeout. New York never got closer than four points the rest of the game. After nearly 30 years in the NBA, the Rockets were finally champions.

During the regular season, Olajuwon had been named the league's Most Valuable Player (MVP). He had also won the Defensive Player of the Year Award. In the finals he had averaged 26.9 points per game. He had outscored Ewing in all seven games. Olajuwon was named Finals MVP. No player in the history of the NBA had ever won all three awards in the same season before.

As the final seconds ticked down, fans started crowding the court. A line of security had to form to keep them from coming onto the floor. When the final horn sounded, some fans did spill over to celebrate with their team. Even in the growing crowd, one player stood head and shoulders above everyone else. Hakeem Olajuwon had finally delivered a championship to Houston.

Houston forward Otis Thorpe holds up the championship trophy after the Rockets beat the Knicks in Game 7.

CHAPTER TWO

HISTORY IN HOUSTON

Houston's NBA story actually began not in Texas but in California. Bob Breitbard wanted to turn San Diego into a hot spot for pro sports. He brought the NBA to town, founding the San Diego Rockets in 1967. The Rockets entered the NBA as an expansion team that year alongside the Seattle SuperSonics.

The Rockets drafted well. They picked up future NBA stars like guard Calvin Murphy, center Elvin Hayes, and forward Rudy Tomjanovich. Despite that, the Rockets made the playoffs only once in their first four seasons.

They also struggled to draw fans. As a result, money was tight. At one point during the 1970–71 season, Hayes refused to take any salary while the team lost 16 of 17 games. It didn't help. By 1971 Breitbard decided to get out of the NBA business. He sold the team to a group of Texas businessmen who moved the Rockets to Houston.

Rockets center Elvin Hayes (11) rises up to block a shot while playing for the San Diego Rockets in 1970.

Moses Malone averaged 17.6 rebounds per game during his MVP season in 1978–79.

During their early years, the Rockets played all over south Texas in hopes of winning over fans. In addition to Houston, they played games in San Antonio, Waco, and El Paso. They even returned to San Diego for a few games.

TEXAS-SIZED BIG MEN

The team's fortunes finally began to change when 6-foot-10-inch center Moses Malone arrived in 1976. The Rockets became a regular playoff team. In 1980–81 their 40–42 record was barely good enough to make the playoffs. But then the Rockets caught fire. With Malone dominating the paint, Houston reached the NBA Finals. The Boston Celtics eventually ended Houston's run. The heavily favored Celtics won the Finals in six games.

Malone moved on before the 1982–83 season. A year later, luck helped the Rockets find their next star center in Ralph Sampson. The 7-foot-4-inch Sampson had been a great college player. At the time, the NBA used a coin flip between the worst teams in each conference to decide the first draft pick. The Rockets were up against the Indiana Pacers. Rockets owner Charlie Thomas called "heads" on the advice of his daughter Tracy. It landed heads, and Houston got Sampson.

A year later, Houston was in another coin flip for the first pick. This time it went up against the Portland Trail Blazers, who picked up Indiana's draft spot in a trade. The Blazers called "tails." The coin again came up heads. The prize of the draft was a 7-foot center from the University of Houston. His name was Akeem Olajuwon. Seven years later he added an *H* to the front of his first name to honor its original Arabic spelling. From then on, he was known as Hakeem Olajuwon.

Olajuwon and Sampson gave Houston "Twin Towers" in the middle. By 1985–86 the Rockets were one of the best teams in the league. They upset the mighty Los Angeles Lakers to earn a spot in the 1986 NBA Finals. Once again, the Rockets faced the Celtics. And once again, the Rockets lost in six games.

The Twin Towers experiment did not last much longer. Houston traded Sampson to the Golden State Warriors in December 1987. The team decided to build around Olajuwon.

Despite his All-Star play, the Rockets didn't improve. They were a playoff team every year. But they had trouble advancing.

CHAMPIONSHIP PIECES

In the middle of the 1991–92 season, the Rockets made another key move. The underachieving team fired head coach Don Chaney. In his place came former Rockets star forward Rudy Tomjanovich.

The move didn't work at first. The Rockets missed the playoffs that season with a 42–40 record. But the next year they improved to 55–27. They lost in the conference semifinals, but Houston was becoming a true contender.

During the early 1990s, the Chicago Bulls were dominating basketball. Behind star guard Michael Jordan, Chicago won three straight titles. But then the rest of the league caught a break in 1993. Jordan unexpectedly retired to try his hand at professional baseball. Houston was one of several great teams ready to take the Bulls' place. Olajuwon was one of the most feared big men in the league.

The pairing of big men Hakeem Olajuwon, *left*, and Ralph Sampson, *right*, set Houston on a winning path in the mid-1980s.

Around him the team had a strong cast of role players. In 1993–94 the Rockets truly blasted off. They won 58 games and claimed their first NBA title by defeating the New York Knicks.

Houston hoped to repeat in 1994–95. But the regular season was a struggle. The Rockets finished 47–35. In February 1995 the Rockets even made a big trade to try to improve the team. In came star guard Clyde Drexler from Portland. Drexler and

Clyde Drexler's arrival midway through the 1994–95 season helped propel the Rockets to another championship.

Olajuwon had been college teammates. Many thought they could rekindle that magic in the pros.

Even Drexler's arrival didn't help at first. The team struggled at the end of the season and had just the sixth seed in the playoffs. That meant the Rockets would have to play most of their postseason games on the road.

It didn't matter. Houston first knocked out the powerhouse Utah Jazz. In the second round, the Rockets rallied from a 3–1 series deficit to beat the Phoenix Suns. Victory over the San Antonio Spurs sent Houston back to the NBA Finals.

The veteran Rockets were matched up with the young, exciting Orlando Magic. The Magic had two of the game's best young players in center Shaquille O'Neal and point guard Penny Hardaway. But Orlando did not have Olajuwon. The veteran taught O'Neal a few lessons during a surprising four-game sweep. Olajuwon outscored O'Neal in each game. His variety of quick jukes and fakes moved the burly Magic center out of the way. Olajuwon was named the Finals MVP after Houston became the fifth team in NBA history to win back-to-back titles.

A NEW GENERATION

Olajuwon eventually left Houston in 2001. The Rockets went looking for their next great big man. This time they found him in China.

Yao Ming grabbed attention for a lot of reasons. First, he was

Yao Ming helped the Rockets reach the playoffs five times during his eight seasons in Houston.

7 feet, 6 inches tall. The towering center had a soft shooting touch and solid passing skills. The Rockets took him with the top pick in 2002.

The jerseys of Yao and teammate Tracy McGrady became best-sellers. But even with the talented pair, the Rockets had trouble breaking through in the loaded Western Conference. Houston won just one playoff series during Yao's eight seasons.

After decades trying to win with the best centers in the league, Houston used a different style to thrive in the 2010s. In October 2012 Houston traded for guard James Harden. He had the ability to shoot from anywhere on the floor. With Harden leading the way, the Rockets were once again playoff regulars.

A new coach, Mike D'Antoni, arrived before the 2016–17 season. D'Antoni preferred a fast-paced game. The Rockets poured in points while winning at least 53 games in each of the next three years. But they still had trouble getting past talented

Streaking Comets

The Rockets weren't the only team to hang championship banners at the Summit. The Houston Comets were one of the first Women's National Basketball Association (WNBA) teams. They were also the first superteam in the league's history. The Comets won each of the first four WNBA titles thanks to stars Sheryl Swoopes, Tina Thompson, and Cynthia Cooper. The success did not last, however. The Comets folded in 2008.

Center Christian Wood emerged as a reliable scorer after joining the Rockets in 2020.

teams like the Golden State Warriors and San Antonio Spurs in the playoffs.

Despite his MVP play, the Rockets never reached the Finals with Harden on the roster. By 2020–21 the team was no longer a contender. Harden asked to be traded nine games into the season. Houston sent him to the Brooklyn Nets. The Rockets went looking for a new star to lead them back to the playoffs.

CHAPTER THREE

ROCKETS AND STARS

Elvin Hayes didn't pick up the game until he was in eighth grade. Even then, it wasn't by choice. A mix-up at Hayes's school ended with a teacher putting him on the team.

The decision changed Hayes's life and the course of Rockets history. San Diego used the top pick in the 1968 draft on the big center. Hayes immediately became the face of the franchise. Using a turnaround jumper that was nearly impossible to defend, Hayes led the NBA in scoring as a rookie.

When the franchise moved to Houston, it was supposed to be a happy homecoming for the former University of Houston star. The party didn't last. Hayes was traded to the Baltimore Bullets a year later. He returned at the end of his career in the mid-1980s.

Guard Calvin Murphy spent his entire 13-year career with the Rockets before retiring in 1983.

Rudy Tomjanovich (45) launches a jump shot against the Baltimore Bullets during a 1973 game.

STARS OF THE 1970s

Hayes was a giant. Point guard Calvin Murphy was not. At just 5 feet, 9 inches tall, Murphy was one of the smallest players in the NBA. Lack of size didn't stop Murphy from becoming one of the league's best guards. Starting in 1970, he spent all 13 seasons of his career with the Rockets. Murphy averaged 17.9 points per game.

Long before he coached Houston to a pair of titles, Rudy Tomjanovich was a star player for the team. The sweet-shooting forward helped Houston become competitive in the 1970s. But Tomjanovich's career nearly ended in 1977 after an ugly on-court incident. He was punched in the face by Kermit Washington of the Los Angeles Lakers. The punch broke Tomjanovich's jaw and several other bones in his face. He missed the rest of the season. But Tomjanovich returned the following year and made the All-Star team.

Moses Malone surprised the basketball world when he made the decision to skip college and go straight to the pros in 1974. The muscular 6-foot-10-inch center came to Houston in 1976. He proved to be the dominant post player the Rockets needed. Where some players gave second and third efforts to get a rebound, opponents said Malone gave nine or 10. Few players rebounded better than the "Chairman of the Boards." His powerful play helped Houston pull off a string of upsets to reach the 1981 NBA Finals. Malone was also a great scorer who averaged 24.0 points per game over six seasons in Houston. Twice during his time with the Rockets, he was named NBA MVP.

THE CONTENDERS

Ralph Sampson was a very different type of center for the Rockets. Most big men stayed near the basket in Sampson's time. But he was just as comfortable taking jump shots as he was dunking. Sampson made the All-Star team in each of his four full seasons with Houston. Injuries cut short his career after he left the Rockets. Sampson was out of the NBA by the time his former teammate Hakeem Olajuwon guided the Rockets to back-to-back titles.

These days the NBA features players from all over the world. That was not the case when Olajuwon joined the NBA in 1984. In fact, Olajuwon's success is part of the reason the NBA is now a league full of global superstars. He grew up in Lagos, Nigeria, playing handball and soccer. The skills he learned while playing those sports

Hakeem Olajuwon posted a double-double in each of his first 12 NBA seasons.

served him well on the court. Olajuwon's quick feet and even quicker hands made him one of the best defensive players in NBA history. He led the NBA in blocks three times and in rebounding twice.

Point guard Kenny Smith was one of the key contributors to the Rockets' two championship teams.

His quick scoring moves were too much for bigger, slower centers to handle. The 7-foot, 255-pound Olajuwon's signature move was the "Dream Shake." He would shrug defenders off with a quick shoulder fake before spinning the other direction for an easy shot. The shake caused nightmares for opponents during Olajuwon's record-setting 18-year career.

Olajuwon was the team's undisputed star in the early 1990s. But he needed help to win NBA titles. The Rockets surrounded him with key role players. Guard Vernon Maxwell and forward Robert Horry provided clutch outside shooting. But point guard Kenny "the Jet" Smith ran Houston's offense. Smith grew up in New York City idolizing Walt Frazier of the New York Knicks. Frazier used to say that great players made a name for themselves in the playoffs. Smith did just that in Game 1 of the 1995 NBA Finals against Orlando. His three-pointer with 1.6 seconds left forced overtime. The Rockets went on to win the game. Seven days later they completed their upset sweep of the Magic.

The 1994–1995 season also saw Clyde Drexler return to Houston. Drexler was an elite NBA scorer. Known as "Clyde the Glide" for his graceful play, Drexler began his career with the Portland Trail Blazers. He even led them to the NBA Finals twice but lost both times. A midseason trade in 1995 brought Drexler to the Rockets. He gave them another elite scorer to take the heat off Olajuwon. The 6-foot-7-inch shooting guard averaged more than 20 points per game during the playoffs. He also led Houston in assists during its amazing run to a second championship.

T-MAC AND YAO

In 2002 the Rockets found another star beyond the borders of the United States. Basketball was popular in China. But Yao

Tracy McGrady, *left*, and Yao Ming, *right*, formed an exciting duo for Rockets fans in the early 2000s.

Ming became the country's first superstar after he was drafted first overall in the NBA Draft.

Yao had a massive 7-foot-6-inch frame, and he had developed elite skills to go with it. By his second NBA season he was one of the best players in the league. Twice in eight years he averaged a double-double. But Yao's influence went far beyond stats. His success broke barriers for other players from China. And his home country followed his every move. During one game in 2007 against a team that had another Chinese player, more than 200 million people in China tuned in to watch. That's nearly 90 million more people than the record for the NFL's Super Bowl.

The Rockets gave Yao a running mate in high-scoring swingman Tracy McGrady. Houston traded for "T-Mac" in

2004. The Rockets hoped McGrady and Yao would give the team an inside/outside duo that would push them deep into the playoffs. It did not happen, but it was tough to blame McGrady. He averaged 22.7 points in parts of six seasons with the Rockets.

FEAR THE BEARD

By the 2012–13 season, the Rockets were again in the market for a star. This time they found one on the bench of one of their rivals. James Harden had been a key substitute for the Oklahoma City Thunder early in his career. But the Thunder had two superstars in forward Kevin Durant and guard Russell Westbrook. Harden thought he could reach that level with more playing time. The Rockets did too. They brought him over in a trade. Harden spent the next eight years lighting up NBA scoreboards. He won the NBA's MVP Award in 2017–18 while averaging 30.4 points per game.

During his MVP season he joined legend Michael Jordan as the only players to average at least 20 points, eight assists, five rebounds, and 1.7 steals per game. Harden's step-back three-pointer became one of the league's toughest shots to guard. And his long, pointy beard made him one of the most recognizable faces in basketball.

During his nine seasons in Houston, guard James Harden was one of the NBA's best scorers.

CHAPTER FOUR

HOUSTON HIGHLIGHTS

The Rockets were in their eighth season—and their second city—when they finally made a playoff memory. The Rockets struggled on the court until finally making some postseason noise in 1974–75.

Back then the opening round was a best of three games. Houston was facing the New York Knicks. In the deciding game, Rudy Tomjanovich poured in 25 points. The Rockets' defense did the rest. The team clamped down on Knicks Hall of Fame forward Bill Bradley in a convincing 118–86 win. It was the team's first-ever playoff series victory.

LAKE SHOWS

Houston's 1980–81 team was not supposed to be a playoff threat—certainly not to the mighty Los Angeles Lakers. But the Rockets had a chance to upset the heavily favored Lakers in

Rudy Tomjanovich was one of Houston's most memorable players in the 1970s, and he later coached the team to a pair of NBA titles.

Game 3 of the first round. Houston trailed by one point late in the fourth quarter. Los Angeles swarmed Rockets point guard Calvin Murphy, thinking he would take the key shot. Instead he dished the ball to guard Mike Dunleavy for an open jumper. The clutch shot put Houston ahead, and the Rockets held on to win the game and the series.

The teams met again in the 1986 playoffs. Houston took a 3–1 series lead into Game 5. The game was tight, and the Rockets had to win without center Hakeem Olajuwon. He had been ejected in the fourth quarter after a fight with a Lakers player.

Houston's other "Twin Tower" stepped up. The game was tied 112–112 with one second left. The Rockets were inbounding in the frontcourt but barely had enough time to get a shot. Sampson took the inbounds pass with his back to the basket. Instead

Ralph Sampson's over-the-shoulder heave stunned the Los Angeles Lakers in the 1986 Western Conference finals.

Rockets fans hold up a banner featuring the team's mid-1990s slogan: "Clutch City."

of turning to shoot, he threw up a desperation heave over his shoulder. The shot was ugly, but the result was beautiful. The ball bounced off the rim and through the net as the buzzer sounded. The Rockets were headed to the NBA Finals.

CLUTCH CITY

The 1993–94 Rockets were on a mission. It was apparent from the start of the season. The Rockets tied an NBA record by winning their first 15 games that year. The last win in that streak came on December 2, 1993. Olajuwon scored 37 points and had 13 rebounds in a victory over the New York Knicks. Six months later, Houston beat New York for its first NBA title.

The Rockets did not seem ready to defend their title a year later. They entered the playoffs as the sixth seed in the Western Conference. In the second round of the playoffs, they were locked in a tight Game 7 with the Phoenix Suns. The game was tied 110–110 with 10 seconds left. Rockets guard Mario Elie was open in the corner for a three-pointer. After he made it, Elie blew a goodbye kiss to the Phoenix crowd.

Houston created another miraculous finish in Game 1 of the 1995 NBA Finals. This time the team had a little luck on their side. Houston trailed 110–107 with 10 seconds left. Orlando Magic guard Nick Anderson missed a pair of free throws that could have sealed the win. But Houston could not secure the rebound. Anderson grabbed the ball and was fouled again. Incredibly, he missed two more shots. This time the rebound came down to Kenny Smith.

After a Rockets timeout, it was Smith who took the ball off the inbounds pass. After a pump fake got his defender in the air, he knocked down a game-tying three-point shot.

That forced overtime, which again came down to the wire.

James Harden drives for two of his 60 points against the Orlando Magic in January 2018.

The teams were tied 118–118 with 5.5 seconds left. The play called for Clyde Drexler to drive to the basket, but his floating shot bounced off the rim. Olajuwon was waiting for it and tipped in the game-winning basket. Houston had won in improbable fashion. The favored Magic never recovered from the loss. The Rockets won the series in a sweep. They became the lowest-seeded team ever to win an NBA title.

SOLO FLIGHTS

On December 9, 2004, Houston trailed the San Antonio Spurs by eight in the final minute. The Rockets seemed doomed to defeat. But Tracy McGrady was ready to save the day. The star forward scored 13 points in 35 seconds. His final shot was a three-pointer with 1.7 seconds left that gave Houston an amazing 81–80 win. McGrady later said the rim felt "really, really big." So big, he couldn't miss.

McGrady's heroics took half a minute. Fourteen years later James Harden stretched his over a full game. "The Beard" was made for the fast-paced, three-point–happy NBA of the 2010s. With a huge arsenal of moves and shots, he could be unstoppable. On January 30, 2018, Harden set a franchise record by scoring 60 points against the Magic. But Harden

Quadruple Up

Hakeem Olajuwon spent the early 1990s carrying the Rockets on his broad shoulders. On March 29, 1990, he did a little bit of everything. Olajuwon became just the third player in NBA history to record a "quadruple double." Olajuwon had 18 points, 16 rebounds, 10 assists, and 11 blocks in a 120–94 win over Milwaukee.

The Rockets made teenage phenom Jalen Green the second overall pick in the 2021 NBA Draft.

also got his teammates involved. He had 11 assists as well. And with 10 rebounds on the night, Harden became the first NBA player to ever score 60 points and record a triple-double in the same game.

With Harden gone from the Rockets by the end of the 2020–21 season, the Rockets were starting over. At the 2021 draft, the team added exciting 19-year-old guard Jalen Green. Houston fans hoped he would be the start of a new era.

TIMELINE

1967

The San Diego Rockets join the NBA as one of two new expansion teams along with the Seattle SuperSonics.

1970

The Rockets draft guard Calvin Murphy and forward Rudy Tomjanovich. They are teammates for over a decade while helping the franchise turn itself into a winner.

1971

A group of Texas businessmen buy the Rockets and move the team to Houston, Texas.

1975

The Rockets beat the New York Knicks 118–86 in Game 3 of the first round of the Eastern Conference playoffs to earn their first playoff series win.

1976

Houston acquires center Moses Malone. Malone goes on to become a star for the Rockets, winning MVP awards in 1979 and 1982 and leading Houston to the NBA Finals in 1981.

1981

Despite finishing the regular season 40–42, the Rockets win three playoff series to reach their first NBA Finals. Houston loses the Finals to the Boston Celtics in six games.

1984

The Rockets select center Hakeem Olajuwon with the first overall pick in the 1984 draft.

1986

Ralph Sampson's spinning jump shot at the buzzer lifts the Rockets past the Los Angeles Lakers and into the NBA Finals for the second time in franchise history.

1993

Houston ties an NBA record by winning its first 15 games.

1994

The Rockets win their first NBA title by beating the New York Knicks in Game 7. Olajuwon leads the way with 25 points, 10 rebounds, and seven assists.

1995

Houston becomes the fifth team to win back-to-back NBA titles by sweeping the Orlando Magic in the NBA Finals.

2002

Houston chooses 7-foot- 6-inch center Yao Ming from China with the first overall pick in the draft. Yao is the first player from a foreign league ever drafted first overall.

2012

The Rockets trade for guard James Harden.

2018

Harden becomes the first player to score 60 or more points in a game while also recording a triple-double when he finishes with 60 points, 10 rebounds, and 11 assists on January 30 against the Orlando Magic.

2021

The Rockets edge the Washington Wizards 159–158 on October 30 to set a franchise record for points in a game. Harden leads the way with 59 points.

FACTS

FRANCHISE HISTORY

San Diego Rockets (1967–71)
Houston Rockets (1971–)

NBA CHAMPIONSHIPS

1994, 1995

KEY PLAYERS

James Harden (2012–21)
Elvin Hayes (1968–72, 1981–84)
Moses Malone (1976–82)
Tracy McGrady (2004–10)
Calvin Murphy (1970–83)
Hakeem Olajuwon (1984–2001)
Ralph Sampson (1983–87)
Kenny Smith (1990–96)
Rudy Tomjanovich (1970–81)
Yao Ming (2002–10)

KEY COACHES

Mike D'Antoni (2016–20)
Bill Fitch (1983–88)
Rudy Tomjanovich (1992–2003)

HOME ARENAS

San Diego Sports Arena
   (1967–71)
Hofheinz Pavilion (1971–75)
Compaq Center (1975–2003)
   Known as:
   The Summit (1975–98)
Toyota Center (2003–)

TRIVIA

CHARITY STRIPE

Calvin Murphy had one of the steadiest hands in NBA history while at the free-throw line. During the 1980–81 season, he set an NBA record at the time by making 78 straight free throws.

FROM DOWNTOWN

Houston set a record for three-point attempts in one game on January 16, 2019. The Rockets put up 70 three-pointers in a 145–142 loss to the Brooklyn Nets. They made 23 for a 32.9 shooting percentage.

CLUTCH

The Rockets' mascot is Clutch the Bear. He is named in honor of the Rockets being nicknamed "Clutch City" during their back-to-back NBA titles.

40–40

The Rockets have had two players score more than 40 points in the same playoff game twice. Eric "Sleepy" Floyd and Hakeem Olajuwon did it in 1988 against Dallas. Olajuwon and Clyde Drexler did it against Utah in 1995.

GLOSSARY

assist
A pass that leads directly to a basket.

double-double
Accumulating 10 or more of two certain statistics in a game.

draft
A system that allows teams to acquire new players coming into a league.

expansion
The addition of new teams to increase the size of a league.

fraternity
A student organization for men on college campuses.

overtime
An extra period of play when the score is tied after regulation.

post
The area around the basket where power forwards and centers usually play.

rebound
To catch the ball after a shot has been missed.

rival
An opponent with whom a player or team has a fierce and ongoing competition.

screen
When an offensive player legally blocks the path of a defender to open up a teammate for a shot or a pass.

steal
To take the ball from a player on the other team.

three-pointer
Any shot taken behind the three-point line.

triple-double
Accumulating 10 or more of three certain statistics in a game.

veteran
A player who has played many years.

BOOKS

Flynn, Brendan. *The NBA Encyclopedia for Kids*. Minneapolis, MN: Abdo Publishing, 2022.

Graves, Will. *NBA's Top Ten Teams*. Minneapolis, MN: ABDO Publishing, 2019.

Mahoney, Brian. *GOATs of Basketball*. Minneapolis, MN: Abdo Publishing, 2022.

ONLINE RESOURCES

To learn more about the Houston Rockets, please visit **abdobooklinks.com** or scan this QR code. These links are routinely monitored and updated to provide the most current information available.

ABOUT THE AUTHOR

Will Graves has worked for more than two decades as a sports journalist and since 2011 has served as correspondent for The Associated Press in Pittsburgh, Pennsylvania, where he covers the National Hockey League, the National Football League, and Major League Baseball as well as various Olympic sports.